Anything is Possible

Humor & wisdom for success and prosperity

◼ HAZELDEN®
Keep Coming Back

Created by Meiji Stewart
Illustrated by David Blaisdell

Anything is Possible
© 2000 by Meiji Stewart

ISBN# 1-56838-386-X

Hazelden
P.O. Box 176
15251 Pleasant Valley Road
Center City, MN 55012-0176
1-800-328-9000
www.hazelden.org

Illustration: David Blaisdell, Tucson, Arizona
Cover design: Kahn Design, Encinitas, California

Dedicated to my family, who mean the world to me:
My mother, Nannette, and father, Richard, Grand Mary, Leslie,
Ray and Scott, Sebastien, Emilie, Skye, Luke, Jake, Nannette,
Cairo and Kamana, and to Jewels, Tom, Fumi, Jocelyne,
Richard and Stephen. And especially to my loving wife Claudia
and to Malia and Tommy (our puddledancers).

Thanks to:
David for the wonderful illustrations. Thanks to Jeff for the
delightful book covers, and, even more, for his and Pete's
friendship. Thanks to Neill, Zane, Regina, Jan, Gay and Jane for
all you do and for being so loving and caring. And a very
special thanks to my mom and dad for encouraging me to
believe in and pursue my dreams.

If you've made up your mind
you can do something,
you're absolutely right.

Neither you nor the world knows
what you can do until you have tried.

If you think you can, you can. And if you think you can't, you're right. *Mary Kay Ash*

Everyone has inside of him a piece of good news.
The good news is that you don't know how great
you can be! How much you can love!
What you can accomplish!
And what your potential is!

Anne Frank

No age or time of life,
no position or circumstance,
has a monopoly on success.
Any age is the right age to start doing!

The great composer does not set to work
because he is inspired, but becomes inspired
because he is working. *Ernest Newman*

Success comes in cans.
I can do this.

Those who act receive the prizes.

Aristotle

Confidence is contagious. So is lack of confidence.

Vince Lombardi

Quit sitting up there in the bleachers.
Come on down on the field. Suit up!
Roll around in the dirt! Take a chance
on missing a pass, fumbling the ball...
That's what the champions are willing to do.

The moment you commit and quit holding back,
all sorts of unforeseen incidents, meetings and
material assistance will rise up to help you.
The simple act of commitment is
a powerful magnet for help.

Napoleon Hill

There comes a moment when you have to stop
revving up the car and shove it into gear. *David Mahoney*

The atmosphere of expectancy is
the breeding ground for miracles.

Rodney L. Parsley

When we give it our all,
we can live with ourselves
regardless of the results.

William Wordsworth

What would you attempt to do if you knew you could not fail? *Dr. Robert Schuller*

The odds are with us
if we keep on trying.

Keith DeGreen

We are what we repeatedly do.
Excellence, then, is not an act, but a habit.

Aristotle

For every pass I ever caught in a game, I caught a thousand in practice. *Don Houston*

If you don't like the scene you're in,
if you are unhappy, if you're lonely,
if you don't feel that things are happening,
change your scene. Paint a new backdrop.
Surround yourself with new actors.
Write a new play—and if it's not a good play,
get off the stage and write another one.
There are millions of plays—
as many as there are people.

Leo Buscaglia

Grand adventures await those willing to turn the corner.

Chinese fortune cookie

To be nobody but yourself in a world
which is doing its best, day and night,
to make you like everybody else
is to fight the hardest battle which
any human being can fight...
but never stop fighting!

e. e. cummings

The privilege of a lifetime is being who you are.

Joseph Campbell

Nothing splendid has ever been
achieved except by those who dared
believe that something inside them
was superior to circumstance.

Bruce Barton

Effort only fully releases its reward
after a person refuses to quit.

Napoleon Hill

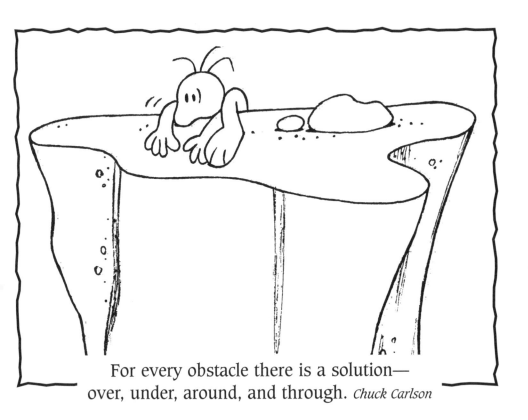

For every obstacle there is a solution—
over, under, around, and through. *Chuck Carlson*

The golden opportunity
you are seeking is in yourself.
It is not in your environment;
it is not in luck or chance,
or the help of others;
it is in yourself alone.

Orison Swett Marden

Nothing is particularly hard
if you divide it into small jobs.

Henry Ford

From a fallen tree, make kindling.

Spanish proverb

We must have courage to bet on our ideas,
to take the calculated risk, and to act.
Everyday living requires courage if life is
to be effective and bring happiness.

Maxwell Maltz

If you wait, all that happens
is that you get older.

Larry McMurty

"But" is a fence over which few leap.

German Proverb

Know what you want to do,
hold the thought firmly,
and do every day what should be done,
and every sunset will see you
that much nearer the goal.

Elbert Hubbard

What lies behind us, and what lies before us
are tiny matters, compared to what lies within us.

Ralph Waldo Emerson

If the future road looks ominous or unpromising, and the roads back uninviting, then we need to gather our resolve and, carrying only the necessary baggage, step off that road into another direction. *Maya Angelou*

The quality of a person's life
is in direct proportion
to their commitment to excellence,
regardless of their chosen field of endeavor.

Vince Lombardi

He can who thinks he can,
and he can't who thinks he can't.
This is an inexorable, indisputable law.

Orison Swett Marden

What I do is prepare myself until I know I can do what I have to do. *Joe Namath*

People rarely succeed at anything
unless they are having fun doing it.

Francois de la Rochefoucauld

Life is always walking up to us and saying
"Come on in, the living's fine,"
and what do we do?
Back off and take its picture.

Russell Baker

Why go into something to test the waters?
Go into it to make waves. *Michael Nolan*

Success Is...

Attitude, more than aptitude

Being happy with who you are

Cultivating, body, mind and spirit

Discovering, that heaven is within

Embracing, the unknown with enthusiasm

Facing fear, finding faith

Giving, without remembering

Here now, breathe into each moment

Inside you, not in people, places or things

Journeying, from the head to the heart

Knowing, your beliefs create your experiences

Letting go, and going with the flow

Making time, for family, friends and forgiveness

Never ever giving up, on your hopes and dreams

Opening your heart, to magnificent possibilities

Passion, playfulness and peace of mind

Quiet time, the key to inspired living

Receiving, without forgetting

Seeking Answers, questioning beliefs

Trusting, in the beauty of your feelings and needs

Understanding, the best you can do is always enough

a *Verb*, choreograph your dance with destiny

Willingness, to learn from everything that happens

Xpressing Yourself, be the hero of your own story

Yours to define, how do you want to be remembered?

Zestful living, loving and laughing

© *Meiji Stewart*

"Begin with the end in mind" is based on the
principle that all things are created twice.
There's a mental or first creation,
and a physical or second creation to all things.

Steven R. Covey

If I have the belief that I can do it,
I shall surely acquire the capacity to do it,
even if I may not have it at the beginning.

Mahatma Gandhi

We are what we believe we are.

Benjamin N. Cardozo

You are the only one who can
stretch your own horizon.

Edgar F. Magnin

We write our own destiny. We become what we do.
Madame Chiange Kai-Shek

A great river is not aimless.
It has direction and purpose.
So also must a good life have definite aim;
all its strength and fullness must
be turned in one direction.

Grenville Kleiser

Don't say you don't have enough time.
You have exactly the same number of hours
per day that were given to Pasteur, Michelangelo,
Mother Teresa, Helen Keller, Leonardo da Vinci,
Thomas Jefferson, and Albert Einstein.

H. Jackson Brown Jr.

Confidence doesn't come out of nowhere. It's a result of something... hours and days and weeks and years of constant work and dedication. *Roger Staubach*

The royal road to success
would have more travelers
if so many weren't lost
attempting to find short cuts.

H. C. Calvin

In order to do something well,
we must first be willing to do it badly.

We learn to do something by doing it.
There is no other way. *John Holt*

What we sow or plant in the soil
will come back to us in exact kind.
It's impossible to sow corn and get a crop of wheat,
but we entirely disregard this law
when it comes to mental sowing.

Orison Swett Marden

Forty thousand wishes
won't fill your bucket with fishes.

Fisherman's Saying

This one makes a net, this one stands and wishes. Would you like to make a bet which one gets the fishes? *Chinese rhyme*

Don't bother about genius.
Don't worry about being clever.
Place your trust in hard work,
enthusiasm, perseverance
and determination.

Sir Frederick Treves

The future belongs to those who
believe in the beauty of their dreams.

Eleanor Roosevelt

Behold the turtle; He only makes progress
when he sticks his neck out. *James Bryant Conant*

You are the architect of your personal experience.

Shirley MacLaine

You see things, and you say, "Why?"
But I dream things that never were,
and I say, "Why not?"

George Bernard Shaw

Reach for the stars—even if you fall short, you will have stretched you potential. *Brenda J. Lauderback*

The biggest human temptation is...
to settle for too little.

Thomas Merton

There are people who put their dreams in a little box
and say, "Yes, I've got dreams, of course, I've got
dreams." Then they put the box away and bring it out
once in a while to look in it, and yep, they're still there.
These are great dreams, but they never even get out of
the box. It takes an uncommon amount of guts to put
your dreams on the line, to hold them up and say, "How
good or bad am I?" That's where the courage comes in.

Erma Bombeck

Cherish your visions and your dreams,
as they are the children of your soul,
the blueprints of your ultimate achievements.

Napoleon Hill

We are what we think.
All that we are arises with our thoughts.
With our thoughts, we make our world.

Gautama Buddha

Don't take yourself too seriously.
And don't be too serious about
not taking yourself too seriously.

Howard Ogden

Procrastination is the art of
keeping up with yesterday.

Don Marquis

That's why many fail—because they don't get started—they don't go. They don't overcome inertia. They don't begin. *W. Clement Stone*

Our greatest danger in life is in
permitting the urgent thing
to crowd out the important.

Charles E. Hummel

Unhappiness is in not knowing what we want
and killing ourselves to get it.

Don Herold

48

Some people reach the top of the ladder of success
only to find it is leaning against the wrong wall.

No great thing is created suddenly,
any more than a bunch of grapes or a fig.
If you tell me that you desire a fig,
I answer you that there must be time.
Let it first blossom, then bear fruit, then ripen.

Epictetus

There are no victories at bargain prices.

General Dwight D. Eisenhower

50

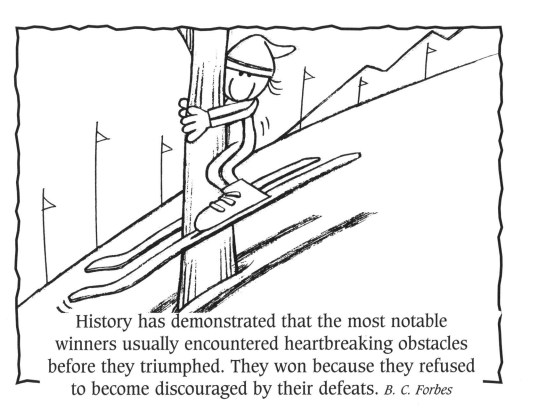

History has demonstrated that the most notable winners usually encountered heartbreaking obstacles before they triumphed. They won because they refused to become discouraged by their defeats. *B. C. Forbes*

Those who dare, do:
those who dare not, do not.

Patrick Dennis

Be ready when opportunity comes....
Luck is the time when preparation
and opportunity meet.

Roy D. Chapin, Jr.

You hit home runs not by chance, but by preparation.

Roger Maris

Just don't give up trying to do
what you really want to do.
Where there is love and inspiration,
I don't think you can go wrong.

Ella Fitzgerald

What you think of yourself
is much more important than
what others think of you.

Seneca

Lots of people want to ride with you in the limo, but what you want is someone who will take the bus with you when the limo breaks down. *Oprah Winfrey*

If you don't know where you're going,
how will you know when you get there?

Casey Stengel

You can be anything you set out to be,
but first you must set out.

Margaret Mead

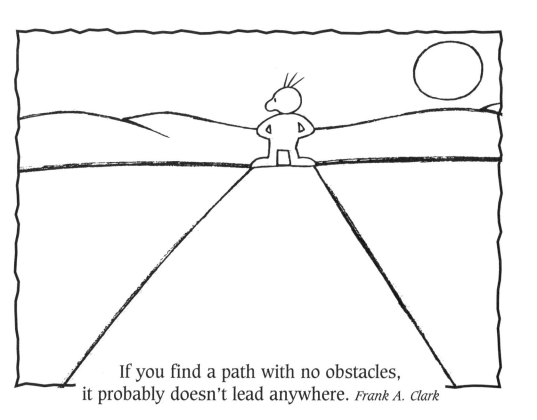

If you find a path with no obstacles,
it probably doesn't lead anywhere. *Frank A. Clark*

Don't listen to those who say, "It's not done that way." Maybe it's not, but maybe you will. Don't listen to those who say, "You're taking too big a chance." Michelangelo would have painted the Sistine floor, and it would surely be rubbed out by today. Most importantly, don't listen when the little voice of fear inside of you rears its ugly head and says, "They're all smarter than you out there. They're more talented, they're taller, blonder, prettier, luckier and have connections..." I firmly believe that if you follow a path that interests you, not to the exclusion of love, sensitivity, and cooperation with others, but with the strength of conviction that you can move others by your own efforts, and do not make success or failure the criteria by which you live, the chances are you'll be a person worthy of your own respect. *Neil Simon*

With ordinary talent and
extraordinary perseverance,
all things are attainable.

Thomas F. Buxton

Irrevocable commitments that offer no loopholes,
no bail-out provisions, and no parachute clauses
will extract incredible productivity and performance.

Robert Schuller

You are the product of your own brainstorm.

Rosemary Konner Steinbaum

If you can see yourself in
possession of your goal,
it's half yours.

Tom Hopkins

60

He who would eat the fruit must climb the tree.
Scottish Proverb

Nothing can stop the man with
the right mental attitude from achieving his goal;
nothing on earth can help the man with
the wrong mental attitude.

Thomas Jefferson

High achievement always takes place
under the framework of high expectation.

Jack and Garry Kinder

I can do it if I truly think I can.
Rev. Norman Vincent Peale

Once you make a decision,
the universe conspires to make it happen.

Ralph Waldo Emerson

Great ideas need landing gear
as well as wings.

C. D. Jackson

64

She didn't know it couldn't be done so she went ahead and did it. *Mary's Almanac*

Your world is as big as you make it.

Georgia Douglas Johnson

There's no thrill in easy sailing
when the skies are clear and blue,
there's no joy in merely doing
things which anyone can do.
But there is some satisfaction
that is mighty sweet to take,
when you reach a destination
that you thought you'd never make.

Spirella

It is kind of fun to do the impossible.

Walt Disney

If it weren't for the last minute,
nothing would get done.

Education is what you get from
reading the small print on a contract.
Experience is what you get from not reading it.

The will to succeed is important, but what's more important is the will to prepare. *Bobby Knight*

You've got to love what you're doing.
If you love it, you can overcome any handicap
or the soreness or all the aches and pains,
and continue to play for a long, long time.

Gordie Howe

The force of the waves is in their perseverance.

Gila Guri

Big shots are only little shots who keep shooting.
Christopher Morley

Your life is like a book. The title page is your name; the preface, your introduction to the world. The pages are a daily record of your efforts, trials, pleasures, discouragements. Day by day your thoughts and acts are being inscribed in your book of life. Hour by hour, the record is being made that must stand for all time. One day the word "finis" must be written. Let it then be said of your book that is is a record of noble purpose, generous service and work well done.

Grenville Kleiser

Would the kid you were be proud of the adult you are?

By working faithfully eight hours a day,
you may eventually get to be a boss
and work twelve hours a day.

Robert Frost

When you come right down to it,
the secret of having it all is loving it all.

Dr. Joyce Brothers

Self-confidence is the first requisite
to great undertakings.

Samuel Johnson

In every triumph there's a lot of try.

Frank Tyger

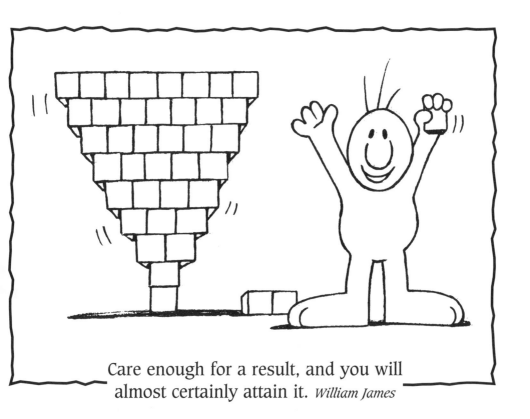

Care enough for a result, and you will almost certainly attain it. *William James*

Far away there in the sunshine are my
highest aspirations. I may not reach them,
but I can look up and see their beauty, believe
in them and try to follow where they may lead.

Louisa May Alcott

When you discover your mission,
you will feel its demand.
It will fill you with enthusiasm
and a burning desire to get to work on it.

W. Clement Stone

Look at a stone cutter hammering away at his rock, perhaps a hundred times without as much as a crack showing in it. Yet at the hundred-and-first blow it will split in two, and I know it was not the last blow that did it, but all that had gone before. *Jacob A. Riis*

In reality, serendipity accounts for 1 percent
of the blessings we receive in life, work, and love.
The other 99 percent is due to our efforts.

Peter McWilliams

Always do your best.
What you plant now,
you will harvest later.

Og Mandino

Many strokes overthrow the tallest oaks. *John Lyly*

Work, work, work and more work is do-do.
Work and relax, work and relax is do-be-do.

Dr. Richard Diamond

It's not half as important to burn the midnight oil
as it is to be awake in the daytime.

E. W. Elmore

I have so much to do that I am going to bed.
Savoyard Proverb

Dare to dream,
dare to try,
dare to fail—
dare to succeed.

G. Kinsley Wood

Ah, but a man's reach
should exceed his grasp.
Or what's a heaven for?

Robert Browning

Goals give purpose. Purpose gives faith. Faith gives courage. Courage gives enthusiasm. Enthusiasm gives energy. Energy gives life. Life lifts you over the bar. *Bob Richards*

To hurry is useless.
The thing to do is to set out in time.

Jean de la Fontaine

It is more important to know where
you are going than to get there quickly.
Do not mistake action for achievement.

Mabel Newcomer

The trouble with life in the fast lane is that you get to the other end in an awful hurry. *John Jenson*

Dare To...

Ask *For What You Want*
  Believe *In Yourself*
Change *Your Mind*
  Do *What You Love*
Enjoy *Each And Every Day*
  Follow *Your Hearts Desire*
Give *More Than You Receive*
  Have *A Sense Of Humor*
Insist *On Being Yourself*
  Join *In More*
Kiss *And Make Up*
  Love *And Be Loved*
Make *New Friends*

Nurture *Your Spirit*
  Overcome *Adversity*
Play *More*
  Question *Conformity*
Reach *For The Stars*
  Speak *Your Truth*
Take *Personal Responsibility*
  Understand *More, Judge Less*
Volunteer *Your Time*
  Walk *Through Fear*
Xperience *The Moment*
  Yearn *For Grace*
be **Z**any

© *Meiji Stewart*

86

We must dare,
and dare again,
and go on daring.

Georges Jacques Danton

We have to dare to be ourselves,
however frightening or strange
that self may prove to be.

May Sarton

87

Potential:
It's all in there.
You've just got to work it out.

Glenn Van Ekeren

People are always blaming their circumstances for
what they are. I don't believe in circumstances.
The people who get on in this world are the people
who get up and look for circumstances they want;
if they can't find them, they make them.

George Bernard Shaw

If you wait for inspiration, you'll be standing on the corner after the parade is a mile down the street. *Ben Nicholas*

The world is what we think it is.
If we can change our thoughts,
we can change the world.

H. M. Tomlinson

The happiest person is the person who
thinks the most interesting thoughts.

William Lyon Phelps

Millions say the apple fell, but Newton was the one to ask why. *Bernard M. Baruch*

Destiny is not a matter of chance;
it is a matter of choice.
It is not a thing to be waited for;
it is a thing to be achieved.

William Jennings Bryan

Listening to your heart is not simple.
Finding out who you are is not simple.
It takes a lot of hard work and courage to
get to know who you are and what you want.

Sue Bender

Never let the fear of striking out get in your way.

George Herman "Babe" Ruth

We are here on earth to do good for others.
What the others are here for,
I don't know.

W. H. Auden

Few speed records are broken by
people who run from temptation.

E. C. McKenzie

If you think you are too small to be effective, you have never been in bed with a mosquito. *Betty Reese*

If you never try you can never succeed. If you try and do the best you can, you will never fail.

Jim Rodgers

Jump into the middle of things, get your hands dirty, fall flat on your face, and then reach for the stars.

Joan L. Curcio

If you can imagine it, you can achieve it. If you can dream it, you can become it. *William Arthur Ward*

To avoid criticism,
do nothing,
say nothing,
be nothing.

Elbert Hubbard

Become a possibilitarian.
No matter how dark things seem to be or actually are,
raise your sights and see possibilities—
always see them, for they're always there.

Norman Vincent Peale

The door of opportunity won't
open unless you do some pushing.

If your real desire is to do good,
there is no need to wait for money before you do it;
you can do it now, this very moment,
and just where you are.

James Allen

People often say that this or
that person has not yet found himself.
But the self is not something that one finds.
It is something that one creates.

Thomas Szasz

It's very important to define success for yourself.
If you really want to reach for the brass ring,
just remember that there are sacrifices that go along.

Cathleen Black

How far would Moses have gone
if he had taken a poll in Egypt?

Harry Truman

Any path is only a path,
and there is no affront,
to oneself or to others,
in dropping it if that is
what your heart tells you.

Carlos Castaneda

Nothing is impossible;
there are ways that lead to everything,
and if we had sufficient will
we should always have sufficient means.

La Rochefoucauld

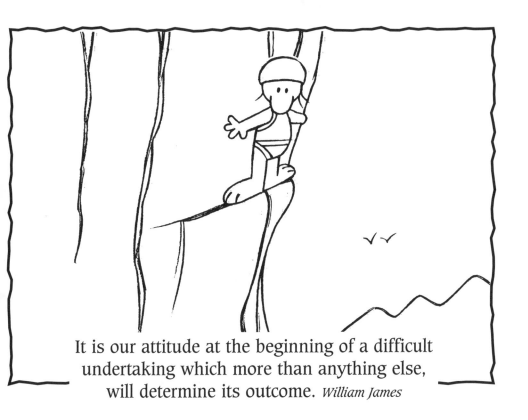

It is our attitude at the beginning of a difficult undertaking which more than anything else, will determine its outcome. *William James*

To know what has to be done, then do it,
comprises the whole philosophy of practical life.

Sir William Osler

Don't fix the blame, fix the problem.

Keith S. Pennington

Act as if what you do makes a difference.
It does. *William James*

We all live in suspense,
from day to day, from hour to hour;
in other words, we are the hero of our own story.

Mary McCarthy

I am a big believer in the "mirror test."
All that matters is if you can look in the mirror
and honestly tell the person you see there,
that you've done your best.

John McKay

You cannot push anyone up the ladder unless he is willing to climb himself. *Andrew Carnegie*

You seldom get what you go after
unless you know in advance what you want.

Maurice Switzer

If Columbus would have turned back,
no one would have blamed him.
Of course, no one would have
remembered him either.

The road to success has many tempting parking places.

Steve Potter

There are no limits to what we can do.
The only limits there are,
are the ones we put on ourselves.

All things are possible.
Pass it on.

Barbara Milo Ohrbach

First say to yourself what you would be,
and then do what you have to do. *Epictetus*

I studied the lives of great men and famous women,
and I found that the men and women who got to the top
were those who did the jobs they had in hand,
with everything they had of energy and enthusiasm.

Harry S. Truman

Undoubtedly,
we become what we envisage.

Claude M Bristol

Luck means the hardships you have not hesitated to endure; the long nights you have devoted to your work. Luck means the appointments you have never failed to keep, the airplanes you never failed to catch. *Margaret Clement*

Every job is a self-portrait of the person who does it.
Autograph your work with excellence.

You only live once—
but if you work it right,
once is enough.

Joe E. Lewis

Love Is...

the *Answer*, whatever the question

Being there, to wipe away the tears

a *Choice*, color the world beautiful

Doing, actions speak louder than words

Everywhere, if you look for it

Forgiving, and for giving

Gratitude, for all that is, was and will be

Holding hands more, hurrying less

Inclusive, not exclusive

Journeying, together on our own paths

Kindness, do what you can when you can

Laughing, listening and letting go

Magical, the more you give, the more you receive

Now, why wait until tomorrow ?

Open-minded, there are many sides to every story

Powerful, be the cause of wonderful things

Quick to build bridges and take down walls

Realizing, you wouldn't want it any other way

Sharing, dare to care

Thoughtful, tender and true

Unconditional, no ifs ands or buts

Vital, like sunshine and rain to a flower

Willingness, to see through the eyes of a child

Xpressing your truth, knowing the answers will come

Yearning, for connection not correction

Zany, dive deep into the mystery

© *Meiji Stewart*

115

Make the most of yourself,
for that is all there is to you.

Ralph Waldo Emerson

When you are inspired by some great purpose, some
extraordinary project, all your thoughts break their
bonds; your mind transcends limitations, your
consciousness expands in every direction, and you
find yourself in a new, great and wonderful world.
Dormant forces, faculties and talents become alive,
and you discover yourself to be a greater person by
far than you ever dreamed yourself to be.

Pantanjali

Yesterday I dared to struggle.
Today I dare to win. *Bernadette Devlin*

Take a chance! All life is a chance.
The person who goes farthest is generally
the one who is willing to do and dare.
The "sure thing" boat never gets far from shore.

Dale Carnegie

Yes, risk-taking is inherently failure-prone.
Otherwise, it would be called sure-thing-taking.

Tim McMahon

Too often, the opportunity knocks, but by the time you push back the chain, push back the bolt, unhook the two locks and shut off the burglar alarm, it's too late. *Rita Coolidge*

Within you lies a power greater
than what lies before you.

Beware what you set your heart upon.
For it surely shall be yours.

Ralph Waldo Emerson

There comes a time in a man's life when to get to where he has to go—if there are no doors or windows—he walks through a wall. *Bernard Malamud*

If at first you don't succeed—
try reading the instructions.

If you keep doing what you've always done,
you'll keep getting what you've always got.

Peter Francisco

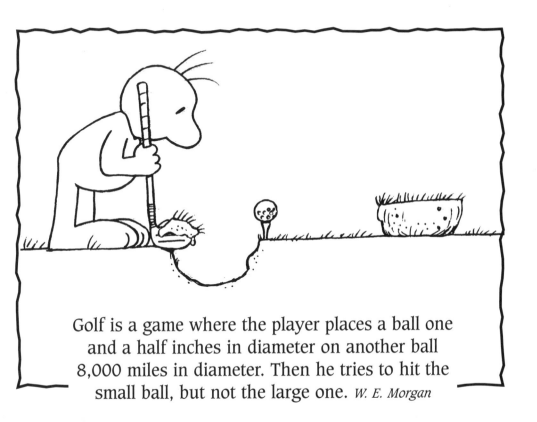

Golf is a game where the player places a ball one and a half inches in diameter on another ball 8,000 miles in diameter. Then he tries to hit the small ball, but not the large one. *W. E. Morgan*

If you want to develop courage,
do the thing you fear to do,
and keep on doing it until you get a record
of successful experiences behind you.
That is the quickest and surest way
ever yet discovered to conquer fear.

Dale Carnegie

All problems become smaller
if you don't dodge them but confront them.
Touch a thistle timidly, and it pricks you;
grasp it boldly, and its spines crumble.

William F. Halsey

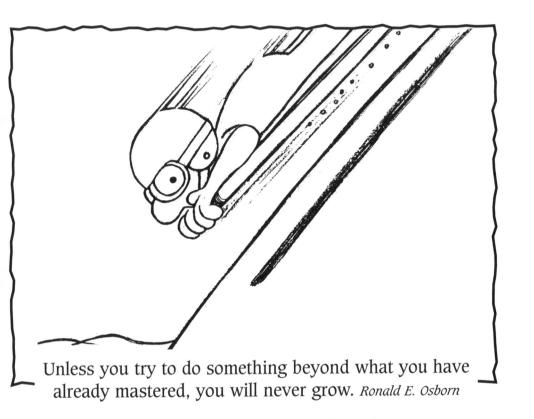

Unless you try to do something beyond what you have already mastered, you will never grow. *Ronald E. Osborn*

My favorite thing is to go where I've never been.

Diane Arbus

Only those who will risk going too far
can possibly find out how far one can go.

T. S. Eliot

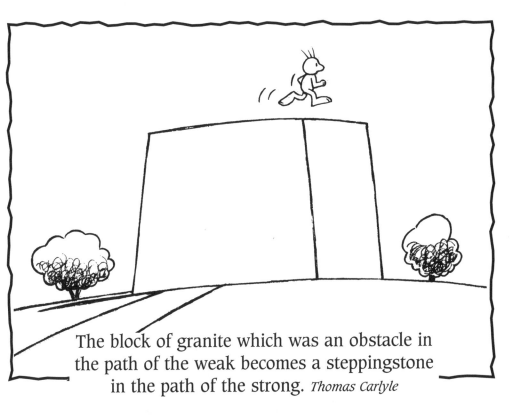

The block of granite which was an obstacle in the path of the weak becomes a steppingstone in the path of the strong. *Thomas Carlyle*

There's a difference between interest and commitment.
When you're interested in doing something,
you do it only when it's convenient.
When you're committed to something,
you accept no excuses, only results.

Kenneth Blanchard

I generally avoid temptation
unless I can't resist it.

Mae West

Every great discovery I ever made,
I gambled that the truth was there,
and then I acted on it in faith
until I could prove its existence.

Arthur H. Compton

I didn't want to quit
and say for the rest of my life,
"Well maybe I could have been..."

Frank Shorter

Ain't no chance if you don't take it.

Guy Clark

It is not because things are difficult
that we do not dare;
it is because we do not dare
that they are difficult.

Lucius Annaeus Seneca

Until you try, you don't know what you can't do.
Henry James

What is the difference between
an obstacle and adversity?
Our attitude toward it.
Every opportunity has a difficulty
and every difficulty has an opportunity.

J. Sidlow Baxter

Opportunity is often difficult to recognize;
we usually expect it to beckon us
with beepers and billboards.

William Arthur Ward

I always tried to turn every disaster into an opportunity.
John D. Rockefeller

Take your mind out every now
and then and dance on it.
It is getting all caked up.

Mark Twain

It's never too late—
in fiction or in life—
to revise.

Nancy Thayer

Keep out of ruts; a rut is something which if traveled in too much, becomes a ditch. *Arthur Guiterman*

I am an optimist.
It does not seem too much use
being anything else

Ralph Waldo Emerson

Risk! Risk anything! Care no more
for the opinion of others, for those voices.
Do the hardest thing on earth for you.
Act for yourself. Face the truth.

Katherine Mansfield

No pessimist ever discovered the secrets of the stars, or sailed to an uncharted land, or opened a new heaven to the human spirit. *Helen Keller*

One needs something to believe in, something for which one can have whole-hearted enthusiasm. One needs to feel that one's life has meaning, that one is needed in this world.

Hannah Senesh

It is good to have an end to journey towards; but it is the journey that matters, in the end.

Ursula K. LeGuin

Make no little plans; they have no magic to stir men's blood...
Make big plans, aim high in hope and work. *Daniel H. Burnham*

Take a look at your natural river.
What are you? Stop playing games with yourself....
Where's your river going? Are you riding with it?
Or are you rowing against it?.... Don't you see that
there is no effort if you're riding with your river?

Carl Frederick

If opportunity came disguised as temptation,
one knock would be enough.

Lane Olinghouse

We go through life pulling on doors marked "push." *Ogden Nash*

Love yourself and realize that
whatever you attempt to achieve in
life is a direct reflection of you.

Joe Greene

Your work is to discover your work
and then with all your heart
to give yourself to it.

Gautama Buddha

Every decision you make indicates
what you believe you are worth.

A Course in Miracles

No horse gets anywhere
until he is harnessed.
No steam or gas ever drives
anything until it is confined.
No Niagara is ever turned into light
and power until it is tunneled.
No life ever grows great until it is
focused, dedicated, disciplined.

Harry Emerson Fosdick

Always bear in mind that your own
resolution to succeed is more
important than any other one thing.

Abraham Lincoln

If you haven't got the time to do it right,
when will you find the time to do it over?

Jeffrey J. Mayer

If opportunity doesn't knock, build a door.

Milton Berle

Imagination is the beginning of creation.
We imagine what we desire;
we will what we imagine;
and at last we create what we will.

George Bernard Shaw

I sometimes say that success just happens.
That's not true. You have to make it happen.
When I make up my mind to do something,
I make sure it happens.
You can't wait for the phone to ring.
You have to ring them.

Lord (Lew) Grade

Dig the well before you are thirsty.

Chinese proverb

May you always have...

Adventures to enrich your soul

Blessings showered upon you

Courage to be yourself

Dreams that come true

Enthusiasm to fuel your passions

Family, friends and faith

Great things to look forward to

Health to live long and prosper

Imagination to soar on the wings of

Joy to color your thoughts

Kind words to share

Laughter to brighten your days

Memories to keep you warm

New horizons to explore

Opportunities to grow

Peace in your heart

Questions to ponder

Reverence for life

Strength to overcome adversity

Time to say, "I love you"

Understanding to care

Values to guide you

Wealth enough to share

Xuberance for your xistence

Youthfulness of spirit

Zest to make a difference

© *Meiji Stewart*

148

If the winds of fortune are temporarily blowing against you, remember that you can harness them and make them carry you toward your definite purpose, through the use of your imagination. *Napoleon Hill*

Twenty years from now you will be more
disappointed by the things that you didn't
do than by the things you did.
So throw off the bowlines.
Sail away from the safe harbor.
Catch the trade winds in your sail.
Explore. Dream. Discover

Mark Twain

How badly do you want it?

George Allen

And will you succeed? Yes indeed, yes indeed! Ninety-eight and three-quarters percent guaranteed! *Dr. Seuss*

Risk

To laugh is to risk appearing the fool. To weep is to risk being called sentimental. To reach out to another is to risk involvement. To expose feeling is to risk showing your true self. To place your ideas and dreams before the crowd is to risk being called naive. To love is to risk not being loved in return. To live is to risk dying. To hope is to risk despair. To try is to risk failure. But risks must be taken, Because the greatest risk in life is to risk nothing. The people who risk nothing do nothing, Have nothing, are nothing, and become nothing. They may avoid suffering and sorrow, But they simply cannot learn to feel, And change, and grow, and love, and live. Chained by their servitude, they are slaves; They have forfeited their freedom. Only the people who risk are truly free.

Above all, challenge yourself. You may well surprise yourself at what strengths you have, what you can accomplish. *Cecile M. Springer*

Friends Are...

Amazing, cherish them

Blessings, acknowledge them

Caring, allow them

Dependable, rely on them

Encouraging, hear them

Fallible, love them

Gifts, unwrap them

Healing, be with them

Important, value them

Juicy, savor them

Kind, delight in them

Loyal, mirror them

Magical, soar with them

Necessary, cultivate them

Optimistic, support them

Priceless, treasure them

Quirky, enjoy them

Rare, hold on to them

Strong, lean on them

Teachers, learn from them

Understanding, talk to them

Vulnerable, embrace them

Warmhearted, listen to them

Xtraordinary, recognize them

Young At Heart, play with them

Zany, laugh with them

© *Meiji Stewart*

All things are possible.
Pass it on.

Barbara Milo Ohrbach

Little gift books, big messages

8313

Keep Coming Back

6608

6456

6460

Little gift books, big messages

6458

6568

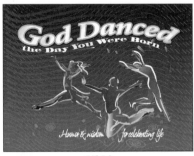

6569

6566

Little gift books, big messages

6457

6570

1737

1736

About the Author

Meiji Stewart has created other gift books, designs, and writings that may be of interest to you. Please visit www.puddledancer.com or call 1-858-759-6963 for more information about any of the items listed below.

(1) **Hazelden/Keep Coming Back** - Over two hundred gift products, including greeting cards, wallet cards, bookmarks, magnets, bumper stickers, gift books, and more. Free catalog available from Hazelden at 1-800-328-9000. To view all the gift products go to www.keepcomingback.com.

(2) **ABC Writings** - Titles include *Children Are, Children Need, Creativity Is, Dare To, Fathers Are, Friends Are, Great Customer Service Is, Great Teachers, Happiness Is, I Am, Life Is, Loving Families, May You Always Have, Mothers Are, Recovery Is, Soulmates, Success Is,* and many more works in progress. Many of these ABC writings are available as posters (from Portal Publications) at your favorite poster and gift store, or directly from Hazelden on a variety of gift products.

(3) ***Nonviolent Communication: A Language of Compassion*** by Marshall Rosenberg (from PuddleDancer Press) - Jack Canfield (*Chicken Soup for the Soul* author) says, "I believe the principles and techniques in this book can literally change the world—but more importantly, they can change the quality of your life with your spouse, your children, your neighbors, your co-workers, and everyone else you interact with. I cannot recommend it highly enough." Available from Hazelden and your local and online bookstores. For more information about the Center for Nonviolent Communication call 1-800-255-7696 or visit www.cnvc.org

▧ HAZELDEN®
Keep Coming Back™

Complimentary Catalog Available
Hazelden: P.O. Box 176, Center City, MN 55012-0176
1-800-328-9000   www.hazelden.org

**Hazelden/Keep Coming Back titles available from your
favorite bookstore:**

Relax, God Is in Charge	ISBN 1-56838-377-0
Keep Coming Back	ISBN 1-56838-378-9
Children Are Meant to Be Seen and Heard	ISBN 1-56838-379-7
Shoot for the Moon	ISBN 1-56838-380-0
When Life Gives You Lemons...	ISBN 1-56838-381-9
It's a Jungle Out There!	ISBN 1-56838-382-7
Parenting...Part Joy...Part Guerrilla Warfare	ISBN 1-56838-383-5
God Danced the Day You Were Born	ISBN 1-56838-384-3
Happiness Is an Inside Job	ISBN 1-56838-385-1
Anything Is Possible	ISBN 1-56838-386-X
Follow Your Dreams	ISBN 1-56838-514-5
Friends	ISBN 1-56838-515-3

Acknowledgments

Every effort has been made to find the copyright owner of the material used.
However, there are a few quotations that have been impossible to trace, and we
would be glad to hear from the copyright owners of these quotations so that
acknowledgment can be recognized in any future edition.